First published by Eulogy For Life 2019

Eulogy For Life
14 Isaacs Street
Busselton, Western Australia 6280
www.eulogyforlife.com

Written by Denise Gibb
Graphic design by Julie Rick
Cover illustration by Austeja Slavickaite

ISBN 978-0-6485446-2-3 (print)
ISBN 978-0-6485446-6-1 (eBook)

Cataloguing-in-Publication data is available from the National Library of Australia.

The Sympathy Gift Series

Healing from Grief
Last Woof
Last Purr
Goodbye Grandma
Goodbye Grandpa

The Sympathy Gift Series offers words of comfort to the bereaved.

Write, email or leave a review online. I'd love to hear how this book comforted you and your family.

sympathygiftseries.com - eulogyforlife.com - denisegibb.com.au

The Sympathy Gift 2 – Last Woof comes to you because you've lost a much-loved canine friend.

Losing your lovable dog brings with it profound heartache and sadness. While there is no right pathway through pet grief, this book will comfort you like a friend.

Filled with uplifting photos and positive affirmations each page comes as a 'last woof'; a reminder from pet heaven to focus on all the happy moments and delightful insights about life your dog has given.

Read from cover to cover, open pages at random, or choose one healing affirmation per day. Over time, each day will become less painful. Memories of your dog will soon fill your heart with warmth and joy, not sadness.

Until then, have faith your dog is in pet heaven wagging his or her tail.

Trust you will get through pet grief. Love, support and many happy barks surround you.

Happy memories are healing memories. (Woof!)

Denise

Paste your favorite photo of your
much-loved dog here.

(Be sure to choose a photo
that makes you smile.)

Every day I promise to walk in honour of my much-loved dog. I will reflect on happy moments and all the delightful insights about having fun and enjoying life my dog taught me.

You only fail when you stop digging.

Good companions don't let you
do stupid things alone.

Just remember, if you get caught, you didn't do it.

Friends buy you lunch,
best companions eat your lunch.

The best thing about happy memories
is making them.

Live in the moment.

If one door closes, and another doesn't open,
try the window.

Take time to 'paws' and relax.

Life is short, focus on happy.

A best friend sits by you when you have nothing
to give but you.

Enjoy the simple pleasures of a walk.

Be proud of your achievements.

Love unconditionally.

Be happy with what you have.

Accept yourself.

You don't have to be perfect to be loved.

Play every day.

A true companion makes it easy to believe in yourself.

Listen more than you bark.

Be fearless for what you want.

Never bite the hand that feeds you.

Live without judgement.

Be loyal and dependable.

Love and be loved.

Appreciate others.

Enjoy the adventure of learning new things.

True friends bring out the best in each other.

Give loyalty to receive loyalty.

Trust, but always verify.

Focus on what you value most.

Greet everyone equally.

Inspire happiness in others.

True friends are together in their hearts forever.

A trouble shared is a trouble halved.

Affection makes the world go around.

Choose faith in yourself over fear.

Never underestimate the power of kindness.

Feelings impact more than words.

Enjoy the little things.

Nothing worth doing is ever easy.

If you never try, you'll never know.

Treasure the love you receive.

10 Tips for Healing Pet Grief

Trust your much-loved dog is in pet heaven. And with each wag of the tail, he or she reminds you to recall all the delightful insights about life given to you. Focus on happy memories while following these 10 tips, and you'll pass through pet grief with courage.

1. Permit yourself to grieve
2. Take care of yourself (ensure a healthy diet balanced with exercise)
3. Allow yourself time
4. Say goodbye and accept your loss
5. Let others help (or ask for help)
6. Help yourself heal from within
7. Prepare for events likely to make you sad
8. Trust you can get through grief
9. Do new things just for you
10. Remind yourself every day; happy memories are healing memories.

Facing each day will become less painful. The memory of your much-loved dog will soon fill your heart with warmth and joy, not sadness. Until then, be sure to connect and talk with family, friends, and colleagues*.

Love and many happy woofs surround you.

(* Should you find yourself at the point where grief is hampering how you live, or it's affecting work or your relationships, please seek professional medical help. Severe long-term grief can put your physical, mental and emotional health at risk.)

About the Author

Denise Gibb is an Australian author whose professional writing draws from a rich tapestry of experience.

She's written with Australia's most trusted psychic medium, Mitchell Coombes, to create bestselling titles like *Sensing Spirit* and *Signs from Spirit*.

When working for ABC Radio Denise wrote *Talking in the Streets*—a ten-part drama awarded a gold medal at the New York Festivals.

From print, radio and television through to social media, Denise has written books, resources, advertisements, digital content and more.

Similarly, Denise's unique personal insight into life after death, balancing success with failure and life with loss led to her creating *The Sympathy Gift Series*.

"My desire is to help people use the energy of happy to heal sad."

Denise currently lives in Australia with her partner.

Write, email or leave a review online. Denise would love to hear how this book comforted you and your family.

Find out more at sympathygiftseries.com - eulogyforlife.com - denisegibb.com.au

CPSIA information can be obtained
at www.ICGtesting.com
Printed in the USA
LVHW071729190720
661082LV00018B/2908